F. SC FITZGERALD

C000076079

SOME SORT OF EPIC GRANDEUR

By Tiziano Brignoli

Copyright © 2020 Tiziano Brignoli.

All rights reserved. No part of this publication may be reproduced, distributed, or transmitted in any form or by any means, including photocopying, recording, or other electronic or mechanical methods, without the prior written permission of the publisher, except in the case of brief quotations embodied in critical reviews and certain other noncommercial uses permitted by copyright law. For permission requests, visit the website tizianobrignoli.it and send a request.

ISBN: 9798680781692 (Paperback)

Printed by Amazon KDP.

First US edition, September 2020.
First Italian edition, January 2019

To nostalgic...

"The past is never dead. It's not even past."

William Faulkner

CONTENTS

Introduction

The figure of Francis Scott Fitzgerald, since his death in December 1940, over the following decades, has been the subject of discussions and sometimes even speculations.

Scott was certainly a man of contradictory characteristics and qualities. He was bold and sarcastic, as he often showed in his literature, especially at the beginning and end of his career. He was ambitious because he was aware of his own talent. The same awareness he assumed when, in 1917, perhaps with presumption, but also with the literary authority that belongs only to people of great destiny, working on his first novel, he told his friend Edmund Wilson, whom he affectionately called "Bunny": "I really believe that no one else could have written so searchingly the story of the youth of our generation."

Scott was, moreover, full of hope—the same hope Gatsby had for the green light at the end of the dock at Daisy's villa—but he was far from being deluded by it. He was humble in his letters—to his editor, to his friends, to his beloved daughter Frances, lovingly called "Scottie", and to his dear Zelda—but suddenly he knew how to appear frivolous and superficial, condemned by the fear of growing old and losing the magic of youth. In the same letter to Wilson he added: "God, how I miss my youth." And he was 20 years old at the time. But as he specified: "That's only relative of course, but already lines are beginning to coarsen in <u>other</u> people and that's a sure sign."[1]

He was boundless in excess and luxury, but modest in living with what he could and had. As he wrote, consciously reviewing his life, he first lived in hectic New York with $36,000 a year (the equivalent of over $450,000 today). Then suddenly, when young American college students seemed to have lost interest in his literature, and the money he wasted was weighing on his shoulders, conditioning his life and writing, he lived on "practically nothing a year."[2] He began to borrow thousands of dollars from his editor and agent to support his life, and consequently his literature. Loans that were then always punctually and rigorously repaid.

Most of all, though, Scott loved writing, and he loved the very act of writing. He devoted himself to it throughout his career as the most important of missions, as the most necessary of purposes.

With his writing he seems to be able to understand you, to tell you that you are not alone in the immensity and coldness of the universe. And you, reading it, seem to be able to understand it in the same way. A sort of primordial human understanding of the meaning of life itself. In his literature, Scott Fitzgerald had the extraordinary talent to bring you face to face with what you were and what you thought you were, questioning your certainties, leaving you free to lose yourself in the eloquence of his words.

He didn't give up when his first novel was rejected twice by the historic publisher *Scribner*. He modified it, changed its structure, and then became known as *This Side of Paradise*.

Many years later, writing to her daughter Scottie, he told her that "Nobody ever became a writer just by wanting to be one." It must be something for which one is willing to sacrifice everything—even his own health. "If you have anything to say, anything you feel nobody has ever said before, you have got to feel it so desperately that you will find some way to say it that nobody has ever found before."[3]

To his "dearest Scottina" he made it clear that writing is a tremendously lonely job, but he was convinced that he knew that world, that he understood it. He knew that it's an honest, even if imperfect world; it's a hard, even if sweet world; a world in which you either immerse yourself completely, holding your breath, or it's better to stay away. Understanding his writing process is fundamental within Scott Fitzgerald's psychological and literary understanding.

His life had lived high on excesses. Above the incoherent lights of New York baldoria and the chic parties on the French Riviera, but they were moments cut out from his beloved writing. Parties and writing. Drinking and writing. Travel and writing. Fights, jealousies, ambitions and writing. For himself and others. He loved literature and the idea of contributing to the development of others' careers, as he did, among others, with whom he considered the "real deal": Ernest Hemingway.[4]

Zelda, three days after her husband's death, aware of how much he first rejoiced at his success, then suffered to find the right words, and always contributed to American literary development, recalled that Scott: "Spent nights on nights working on other people's manuscripts, moving paragraphs and giving some good advice, even when he was too sick to take care of himself."[5]

I

A character's profile

In the spring of 1933, late at night, F. Scott Fitzgerald, talking to a guest who visited him in his Baltimore apartment, said: "Sometimes I don't know whether Zelda and I are real or just characters in one of my novels."[1]

The most important aspect of Fitzgerald's psychological and literary understanding, in fact, is his own life. Taking into consideration all his writing over the course of his twenty-year career we discover that within his relational and emotional circle he found the most intricate and authentic essence of his writing. Fitzgerald was the protagonist of himself.

Another aspect that it's important to examine it is his capacity for analysis. He was able to observe life in a cynical, direct and sometimes ruthless way. He stripped it naked and made it comprehensible in all its facets. At first happy and exuberant and then sad and melancholic. Light-hearted, thoughtful—real. No writer of the *Généra-*

tion Perdue[1] had such an understanding of the society of the time, the rhythm of its excesses and the sweetness of its desires, the environment and the heartbeat of life. The writer Paul Rosenfeld, in 1925, shortly before *The Great Gatsby* was published, said that the reason for this was that Scott Fitzgerald "knows how talk sounds, how the dances feel, how the crap-games look."[2] He looked at you looking for a story and actually found within you the illusion and power of American living. With the arrival of the new post-war decade—the 1920s—Fitzgerald was well aware of what the country was going to face: a huge, restless, incoherent hangover. "America was going on the greatest, gaudiest spree in history" he wrote many years later. "And there was going to be plenty to tell about it."[3]

For Fitzgerald, moreover, writing was such in its highest artistic and cultural expression. For him, writing meant achieving a social aspiration, but it was also a necessity, an outlet for the pain of life.

His prose was conceived according to an elaborate, well thought and well structured rhythmic elegance. Brilliant, intelligent and conscious in the exposition of his thoughts. This was due to an aspect of his personality that many of his friends, including Hemingway himself, gave him credit for: reflexivity. It was something that when

---

[1] *Lost Generation.* The meaning we give today to this terminology was conceived by Gertrude Stein and then made popular by Ernest Hemingway in *A Moveable Feast.*

you watched in action in all its purity captured you, enchanted you, surprised you and made you believe in the authenticity of his thought.

Fitzgerald knew how to understand and evaluate an event, a state of mind, making it his own, and then significantly detaching himself from it. As he himself wrote in an essay in 1936: "The test of a first-rate intelligence is the ability to hold two opposed ideas in the mind at the same time, and still retain the ability to function." Words that outlined all the components of his adult life: parties and excesses; money as the primary source of desire and illusion; his literature; Zelda herself.[4]

Gerald Murphy, a friend of the Fitzgeralds, who together with his wife Sara made life in Paris and in the French Riviera in the 1920s the real cultural and social centre of expatriate Americans, remembered how Scott had the unique ability to express his thoughts. There were times in particular when "he wasn't harassed" but was only Scott Fitzgerald in the company of other people. And at that moment "he'd tell you his real thoughts about people, and lose himself in defining what he felt about them." And it was in those moments that you could see the true essence of his character. You noticed "the beauty of his mind and nature, and they compelled you to love and value him."[5]

Scott also possessed a deep-rooted sense of values—moral and social values—and was certainly a generous person to others. As Fitzgerald scholar Brian Railsback recalled to the present author, the problem was that, "despite his best intentions, however, he often lacked personal discipline." According to Railsback, the wealth he accumulated at a young age, his excessive use of alcohol and his turbulent relationship with Zelda gradually led him to lose control of his own life.[6]

Scott also possessed a natural talent for understanding the ambiguity of life and human relationships. Despite this, he was always on the constant and forced search for informations and details that could give him a great story.

Particularly during the writing of his fourth novel, *Tender is the night,* he put a lot of attention in recognizing details of life lived by his friends, the Murphys in particular, to be included in the book. Sometimes he might even appear indifferent to his friends. All in order to produce a literary story that was as authentic, original and often autobiographical as possible.

Fitzgerald was also a person who understood what he wanted, and his place in future American literature, and it was there that the many contrasts in his personality were born. He was greedy for success, but he could be humble. Sometimes he was incoherent and superficial, but he knew how to be kind and present, dispensing advices and suggestions to colleagues and friends, even when he was too weakened by his precarious physical health and the most dangerous demon, from whom he made a desperate return: alcohol.

What's certain is that he loved being in the spotlight. "Scott couldn't bear to be ignored," recalled Gerald Murphy. When that happened, he would try so hard to capture the attention of people around him, and he would do so at the expense of anything else. He might even become arrogant and annoying. He was the protagonist! "If he felt that Sara was not paying enough attention to him, he would try to irritate her, or even revolt he," Murphy said. Once they were all in a taxi—Sara, Scott, Zelda, and the American composer Theodore Chanler. Scott, unnerved by their lack of attention for him, suddenly took some filthy old hundred-franc notes and put them in his mouth, chewing them, literally. This was Scott Fitzgerald at the time, on his voracious climb to success.7

When he was, unconsciously, at the end of his extraordinary and cinematic life, he wrote a letter to his daughter Scottie who was studying at Vassar College. "I'm not a great man," he told her, "but sometimes I think the impersonal and objective quality of my talent and the sacrifices of it, in pieces, to preserve its essential value has some sort of epic grandeur."8

2

The new vibrant literary voice

of the Jazz Age

When Scott started writing his first novel he did so, certainly, placing important literary expectations in it, but he also devoted himself to its writing to create the conditions for him to live the life he knew was waiting for him at the corner of the new American decade.

For Fitzgerald, his first book was a project as dear to him as it was important in terms of future prospects. First of all, it must be understood that for Scott, writing has always been a set of conditions that came together, producing in the end a tormented existence that served as a backdrop for his literature. He started writing with the intention of doing it in a big way, and to publish the novel that could possibly change the very conception of literature in America. He did so, also and above all, as a way to conquer the woman who could mark an entire American generation with him. An exuberant woman from the South, of a different beauty and above all intriguing, intelligent, bold, lively and jaunty. Her name was Zelda Sayre.

In September 1919, when *Scribner* accepted his first book for publication, Scott lived in St. Paul, Minnesota, and wrote happily to a friend of him, showing all his character of the time: exuberant, funny, bright and incredibly vibrant, like the music of those years. At the top of the letter, just below his postal address, he added more details about his place of residence:

"In a house below the average,
On a street above the average,
In a room below the roof."

After telling her about the important literary novelty, he exclaimed: "Ain't I smart!"[1]

This Side of Paradise is the name of his first novel, published in 1920, which was conceived and skillfully shaped after his life of the time and the environments he frequented. Over time it became considered not only the book that launched his career and the artistic expression of society at the time in the form of literature, but a true fictionalized autobiography of Scott Fitzgerald. For this reason, *Paradise* still remains an essential reading for all those who aspire to find and understand the thoughts and moods of the first Fitzgerald that America had the opportunity to read and know. He himself, at the tender age of twenty-three, a newly published author, on the lush crest of success, wrote that he was not interested in talking about himself, because after all he had already done so in his book. "To write it took three months; to conceive it—three minutes; to collect the data in it—all my life," he said.

This book gave rise to the idea of Fitzgerald as the author who first knew how to frame the new American generation. Young, and lushly impulsive and rebellious; noisy and redundant in spending its days; sometimes brash, intellectual and interested in the joy and excess of life. A generation that left the classrooms of prestigious American Ivy League colleges and moved to country clubs, and to the loudest and most thunderous, liveliest and most alcoholic parties. "My whole theory of writing I can sum up in one sentence," he boldly wrote. "An author ought to write for the youth of his own generation, the critics of the next, and the schoolmasters of ever afterward."[2]

As soon as the novel was published, what was immediately evident to the critical eye was the willingness of the new and predominant American literary voice to tell what was dear not only to young Harvard, Yale, or

Princeton students,[2] but basically to any kind of man. Wrote the *Harvard Crimson*: the pleasure of enjoying life. "The story is a little slice carved out of real life, running over with youth and jazz and sentiment and romance and virile American humor." In short, concluded the *Crimson*, these are values dear to "any kind of man."

Scott Fitzgerald was therefore the new, vigorous, vibrant voice of jazz, or rather, what jazz at the time represented: the exuberant, easygoing American future whose rhythm would accompany the nation's economic boom in those years.

Harry Hansen, writer, journalist and editor of the *Chicago Daily News*, approved the book, announcing to readers that he would support it to the end as "true writing." [3] Despite some sporadic criticism of the book—columnist Franklin P. Adams described it as "sloppy and cocky"—it was critically acclaimed. Sure, in his early writing there was a certain conceit and literary snobbery, but it was also incredibly funny, self-deprecating and autobiographically sarcastic. Journalist and essayist Henry L. Mencken was one of the many who applauded the author. "Original in structure, extremely sophisticated in manner, and adorned with brilliancy."[4] All qualities with which Fitzgerald led you to reconsider the past and to look with a new eye at the future.

---

[2] Princeton was the university attended by Fitzgerald and then used as a reference in the novel.

The interest in the novel also derived from the use of an elegant, romantic and almost poetic prose, which served to best express the thought that the college students of the East Coast had towards those same environments so well described by the young writer from St. Paul.

This Side of Paradise one can easily considered the most literary novel of the American author. During the course of the book there are in fact numerous and sophisticated conversations between the protagonists that touch upon themes that give the discussions a stimulating and intellectual, ironic and then sometimes even dramatic aspect.

In his early literary productions, his writing may sometimes appear all too slow, but Fitzgerald had the extraordinary talent to suddenly break the rhythm, bringing unexpected changes of scenery and perspective to the story. More simply, Fitzgerald understood the rhythm of his stories.

What made *Paradise* unique and different from the other books he produced? It was autobiographical, of course, as *Tender is the Night* fourteen years later. He looked deep into American society, something Scott also did in *The Great Gatsby*. The uniqueness of this book was precisely the collegial environment in which the story flowed. Here Scott gave free rein to his recent past and his dreams for the near future. He praised and at the same time criticized the Princeton university environment, describing life inside and then outside of college. Above all, he described in an extraordinarily honest and incisive way the life that the new American generation was going to lead. In a 1931 essay he analyzed some of the characteristics that the Jazz Age had brought with it, including one particularly indicative of *Paradise*: "Adolescents lead very amorous lives."[5]

Moreover, in this first book he immediately demonstrated his remarkable capacity of expression, and it's precisely on this subject that it's important to pay particular attention.

Fitzgerald's ability to display scenes, to develop the emotional and relational development of his protagonists, and how he was able to do this in just a few pages, is well recognized. He had the gift of synthesis despite a romantic and incredibly eloquent language. Brian Railsback recalled to this author that Scott's literature, in its best expression, "tended to be lyrical, impressionistic... Even Hemingway admitted Scott's absolute mastery of language."[6] This can be seen in particular in his most famous novel, *The Great Gatsby*, which runs in about 50,000 words. It's a significant and particularly surprising fact how Fitzgerald managed to produce one of America's most beloved novels within such a few words.

For a long time it was a matter of debate whether Fitzgerald had talent in producing screenplays for Hollywood as well. From the beginning of his literary career he had an interest in this area. In 1919, while he was completing his first novel, he wrote to his agent Harold Ober: "Is there money in writing movies? Do you sell scenarios?"[7]

One aspect of his literature that went out of tune with cinema was the dialogue. Almost one hundred years after the release of his first book and numerous cultural and linguistic changes, the way Scott made his protagonists talk can now easily appear forced, artifact, unnatural, particularly when compared to modern novels. In fact, Scott found his literary greatness in all of this. He was able to infuse the protagonists with an emotional and sentimental depth difficult to find in any other book ever written.

Some aspects dear to the new American society were represented in *Paradise*. Universities, or rather, colleges—a purely Ivy League concept—seen more as an artistic, social, cultural centre in which to express and find oneself, rather than just a student centre. Princeton, according to the author, was "The pleasantest country club in America."[8]

During the course of the book the reader comes across student dances and social events in which to get to know America's young, bright, independent and sometimes even impertinent flappers. Women who wanted to symbolize their femininity and their autonomy from the male sex by demonstrating that they could drink, behave, talk just like men. The old taboos were broken, alcohol was the favorite drink, and consequently attitudes were less judicious. Those same flappers that the American author drew on inspiration and enchantment towards his future wife and first American flapper.

Zelda was fascinating because she was different—modern and innovative—and was well known in the exclusive environments of American country clubs. She lacked constancy in her behavior; she was bored with life and excessive morality. In Zelda, Scott found the perfect companion with whom to share adventures and moods that symbolized the new golden door America was approaching. If she didn't always look beautiful—at least not in the literal sense of the word—she was certainly terribly attractive. It seemed endowed with the grace of the past and the irreverence of the future. Zelda and Scott were both attracted and rejected by the boundless grandeur and turbulence of their character. Brian Railsback described Zelda as "the love of his life and a great source of inspiration and tension that he needed to feed himself as a writer."9 If Scott was the male protagonist of his novels, Zelda was certainly the female protagonist.

At the time of their first meeting, in 1918, she lived in Montgomery, Alabama, quite far from New York, where Fitzgerald lived. A distance that was difficult to bridge when considered in terms of money spent on gasoline or taxis. Scott recalled in an interview in 1923: "Especially when the man in question is working—or trying to—on the munificent salary of $35 a week." However, he added, "that was before I started to write—oh yes!"[10] Two years later, when *This Side of Paradise* was published, it sold 3,000 copies in just three days—an instant bestseller.[11] In conclusion, 50,000 copies were sold through twelve prints—certainly much more than a skeptical *Scribner* originally thought it would get.[12]

In a 1937 essay Fitzgerald told of his success at an early age, and how from one year to the next—from 1919 to 1920—every aspect of his life changed dramatically. The previous year he earned $800 from his writing, apparently already a very good profit, except for the $18,000 earned the following year, divided between his first novel, short stories and film rights. These last numbers even represented a small amount compared to what he earned during the economic boom of the decade.[13]

Scott consciously grasped in his own hands the lightness that jazz provided at the time and skillfully transformed it into literature. Just over a week after the publication of *Paradise* he and Zelda got married in St. Patrick's Cathedral in New York City. The most extraordinary American spree ever officially had its protagonists. Intelligent, full of vitality, eccentric, drunk on fun and beyond.

3

Narrate life

Fitzgerald was capable of giving an immortal imprint to the scenes he described, dipping them with a new social awareness. He was able to create new terminologies that later became commonplace and which we now use alongside the Fitzgerald image. When this did not happen, he was able to make those already existing known, popular, discussed, emblematic. One above all, the term *flapper*.

This word previously had a negative and ambiguous connotation, which was used to define vulgar women of low social and moral standing. All this changed with Scott's writing, which from his first novel gave to the word a more popular, accessible, democratic essence within everyone's reach. An adjective that with the meaning Fitzgerald gave was a perfect fit for all those women who wanted to be a bit brash, surely bold, a bit silly, but certainly not *naive*. In two words: Zelda Sayre.

Zelda herself believed that a flapper was a woman who

was not intimidated by others, especially men: fearless and full of vitality. A woman in search of her own expressiveness, of the uniqueness of her character, not dictated by the prototype of femininity, but of femininity as artistic expression.

This latter aspect was something very dear to her husband Scott in his novels and short stories. In his stories, in fact, the women took on the main role—the heroines of the story—those who with an attitude that was at first affectionate, romantic, sweet and then suddenly detached, incoherent and inconsistent influenced the story itself. Fitzgerald simply made women an integral and predominant part of his literature. In all of his four most important novels the role of the female protagonist becomes fundamental in the emotional and psychological development of the male one.

In an interview published in 1923 by Louisville's *Courier-Journal,* the perfect representation of the Scott and Zelda Fitzgerald Show was staged. Fast and pressing jokes with a humorous and lively touch.

The newspaper wondered if Zelda represented "the living prototype of the kind of femininity known as American flapper."

Based on the features of this intriguing woman, full of flair and unconventionality, originally from Alabama, in the warm South of the country, the flappers had to be "reckless and unconventional, because of their quest in search of self-expression."

These women practiced golf and swimming; they listened Jazz music "because it is artistic"; they danced for its sheer abandon. To be clear, they had no interest in being part of a group, but simply enjoying life to the fullest of their possibilities.

Zelda at one point focused on the "heroines" of her husband's books. "That's why," she said, "I love Rosalind in *This Side of Paradise*": the heroine of femininity during the rhythm of jazz. "I like girls like that," she said, shaking a curly crop of honey bobbed hair, just like Scott's. He loved them because they had "courage," because they were "recklessness," but mostly because they were "spendthrift." A set of qualities that made Rosalind, the female protagonist of the book, "the original American flapper." So Zelda, on whom Rosalind was portrayed, in the common imagination became the American flapper par excellence.[1]

Zelda was her husband's main source of inspiration throughout his career. In 1921 Frances "Scottie" Fitzgerald was born, and in the moment her daughter came into the world, "Zelda said, 'Oh, God, I'm drunk. I hope she is beautiful, a beautiful little fool'" recalled Eleanor Lanahan, Fitzgeralds' niece. As we know today, those words were used by Scott for one of *The Great Gatsby*'s most emblematic exclamations. "He recycled almost everything she said. He used her as a model for his heroines."[2]

What were the roaring '20s if not years of excess, exuberance and bravado? Illusional years of perpetual American greatness, and as we shall see later, of Fitzgeraldian greatness itself. These were years when parties in American villas and luxurious hotels in glittering New York became everyday life. The parties were noisier and the drinks were wilder, with two absolute and indisputable protagonists: Scott and Zelda Fitzgerald. It's a consequence of this, then, that both will always be reproduced by collective thinking, Eleanor Lanahan said: "As the footloose adventurers who rode down Fifth Avenue on the tops of taxicabs, danced on tables at the Waldorf and took their famous plunge in the fountain at the Plaza or who partied in Paris."3

It's important to pay attention to this. Scott didn't talk about parties. He organized those same parties. He didn't talk about exciting trips to Europe and the thrill of New York life: he was at the center of that dance floor. He himself was the most bubbly and striking protagonist.

Scott and Zelda, together, provided the 1920s with a certain frivolity, lightheartedness, which started in their youth and continued towards their desire to have fun.

Some time after they got married they moved to the Commodore Hotel in St. Paul, and to say "hello" to their arrival in town they decided to spend half an hour walking through the sliding doors of the hotel. Can you imagine their happiness, their joy, their grace in doing something so simple, futile and joyful?

Jealousy was also part of their character. Once Zelda, while Scott was too focused on talking to a dancer rather than paying attention to her, jumped down a flight of stairs. Once again Scott threw a glass of Murano glass wine against a wall garden during a party organized by Sara Murphy. After an argument, out of jealousy or simply to draw attention to himself, whatever the reason, excesses were part of their life and their desire to mark an era with their name.[4]

Scott and Zelda believed that youth provided them some kind of "right to have fun," to the abuse and abundance of life. Once, while they were on the French Riviera, Zelda left a party she was attending with her husband, took off her evening gown, and jumped into the water from a cliff. Scott was visibly worried but unwilling to admit it, so, as many times in his life, he was conditioned by his wife's character and behavior and dived in turn. When Sara Murphy tried to tell Zelda it was dangerous, the joyous American flapper simply said, "But *Say-ra*, didn't you know? We don't believe in conservation."[5] The more risky, excessive, and noisy it was, the more daring the interest became, the more intense the attraction.

Dorothy Parker, a writer and friend of the Fitzgeralds, on another occasion, after seeing them running around New York City in a taxi, wrote: "They did both look as though they had just stepped out of the sun. Their youth was striking. Everyone wanted to meet them."[6]

It is commonly believed that the author of the disillusioned young Americans coined the term *Jazz Age* but it's not actually correct. This terminology was used, albeit in other contexts and never so representative of the American golden decade, in some books and texts from 1919 to 1921. Fitzgerald in 1922, to accompany the release of his second novel, *The Beautiful and the Damned*, also published a collection of short stories entitled *Tales from the Jazz Age*, and this is where every discussion and interest about this historical period began.

Scott was therefore not the first to conceive this term, but he was the first to contextualize it in such a profound way. He was the first to identify a beginning and an end, and to understand how the rhythm of jazz perfectly matched the rhythm of American lives in those years. Fitzgerald's great capacity for analysis during that decade was to see its end when no one was paying attention to it yet. When it was still in its maximum and striking fervor he began to live it with nostalgia because he was aware that he was part of the illusion of a fleeting moment in history, as fast as a flutter of wings, with the tragic future waiting for him and the past that would never return.

This was something that was dear to Scott. In fact, all his books are marked by a rhythm of life that is too pressing, too voracious, that devours the protagonists and leaves them disenchanted. Nostalgic of the past, of the glorious days when the only worries were drinking and what parties to attend, increasing more and more the tones of life, waking up one morning suddenly tired in body and mind.

In May 1931, when the disillusionment of life had descended on American existence, accompanied by economic collapse, Scott wrote a letter to Max Perkins, his editor, mentor and above all friend. He made it very clear that "the Jazz Age is over" and took the "credit for naming it so and that it extended from the suppression of the riots of May Day, 1919 to the crash of the stock markets in 1929—almost exactly one decade."7

Ten years that for Scott and Zelda meant an alternation of life between the increasingly expensive and wild life in New York to travels in Europe and the much loved and sophisticated French Riviera. All, as always, seasoned and accompanied by writing—painful, intense and daily.

Two years after the collapse of the stock markets Scott analysed the past decade, aware that he had succeeded in his purpose: to tell the '20s in all its inconsistency and diversity. A colorful era in the brightest tints; noisy and frenetic. Nostalgia for the past was overwhelmed by an uncontrolled hope for the future. The people of the Jazz Age seemed to pay no attention to regrets, dedicating themselves exclusively to luxury and excess. Scott, however, observed this more deeply. He wrote that he looked at it with nostalgia, an era that "It bore him up, flattered him and gave him more money than he had dreamed of, simply for telling people that he felt as they did."[8]

This is an important introspective analysis on his part. Fitzgerald in those years was aware that he was playing the role of a friend, a partner in a society that saw in him, itself. If he could exist in such an extraordinary existence, they could exist in it in the same way.

On *This Side of Paradise*, Fitzgerald started everything that we will find in his next writing. He defined people, described concepts, developed thought styles, ways of living. One term he adopted was *slicker*. They were elegant, sophisticated people. Amory Blane, the protagonist of the book, said that the signal to recognize them was, in fact, when "a fellow slicks his hair back with water." But behind this terminology was more than just how to comb one's hair. It symbolized social status. Continuing the description Amory points out that slickers were "good-looking" or even better, "*clean*-looking." People not only intelligent, but with a "social brain," in short, someone well aware of the social rules and conventions of the world—of conversation, but also of presence and appearance. Someone who dresses well, in a clean, elegant, tidy way. Consequently, someone who, through dressing well, finds the most emblematic source of education, prestige, high social status. Someone who uses his intelligence to "be popular, admired, and never in trouble."[9] A description that fits in well with what Scott was at the time. A man who, despite his young age, was already navigated, aware of his own values—social values, which became cultural values. Through the word *slicker*, Fitzgerald wanted to represent all those who knew how to speak, what to say and when to say it, who knew how to dress and why to dress in a certain way. *Slickers*, then, were sophisticated men, refined in their attitudes. They were nothing more than the new American society that found a home in colleges like Princeton, Yale and Harvard.

If we go on for a few decades, in a new American era—the '50s and '60s—we discover that young men who studied in Ivy League colleges, attending the most prestigious clubs, the most exclusive organizations, and then debuting in society, still possessed a character that was perfectly within the term *slicker*. Well-behaved and well-thought out, well-dressed and well-combed, skillful in their human evolution and cunning in their social approval.

4
Short stories

F. Scott Fitzgerald is commonly known as the most iconic and representative novelist of the Jazz Age, and one of the greatest literary protagonists of all time. This greatness came not only from his novels, but also from the many short stories he wrote that marked an important as well a fundamental part of his life as a writer.

During his twenty-year career a collection of short stories was published to accompany each of his novels. This had a very specific purpose. It served to "set" the reader within the context that he would later find in a much more important book. Sometimes they were just drafts to be expanded, rejected by publishers. Other times they were great stories published in the *Saturday Evening Post*. In any case, reading them carefully, you can perceive Fitzgerald's predisposition to use them as land to cultivate and then build a final novel. In 1933, Scott wrote to his wife, who was hospitalized because of her increasingly frequent nervous breakdowns, and recently wrote the book *Save me the Waltz*, about his success as a writer. He felt clearly oppressed and somewhat obstructed by Zelda's talent—at the very beginning wife, then partner and finally rival. "I am the highest paid short story writer in the world," he wrote to her, to emphasize his greatness, what he believed to be real literary greatness. He certainly didn't write it with humility, but he didn't say anything wrong. In 1929, in fact, Fitzgerald was paid $4,000 a story, the equivalent of $55,000 today.[1] For a single story.

During his two decades of career, Fitzgerald has not always been consistent in writing novels. From his third publication, *The Great Gatsby*, to the next and final one, *Tender is the Night*, nine years passed. In his lifetime he published only four novels[3], but wrote about 180 short stories.[2] Consequently, much of his talent is to be analyzed in short literature, and how this had an impact on his most prestigious works of writing.

It's interesting, however, how Fitzgerald didn't like to write short stories, because according to him they were a kind of intellectual prostitution necessary to earn money in a short period of time—money he would have needed to spend more time writing a novel, instead of writing "garbage" that people like. For him, some of the stories he

---

[3] *The last Tycoon* remained unfinished after his death in 1940 and was published the following year by his friend and literary critic Edmund Wilson. For many, it was a masterpiece.

wrote were simply "hack work"—banal, uncreative work.3 In particular, he complained to Max Perkins, because: "The more I get for my trash the less I can bring myself to write."4 A relationship of love and hate, because, to be clear, Fitzgerald had a natural talent for writing short stories. Short stories from which he would later took some piece here, some piece there for his novels, particularly *The Great Gatsby* and *Tender is the Night*. The names of the protagonists changed, sometimes the general plot, but the underlying set design, the heartbeat that gave the rhythm to the whole story, often found great similarities.

The diamond as big as the Ritz (published in the collection *Tales of the Jazz Age*, 1922) is a story with almost surreal fictional connotations, but certainly one of the most significant to describe the reality of that American decade.

It's a story about wealth—a such wealth that it's hidden from the American government. A wealth so immense that it becomes an obsession, that it conditions attitudes and judgments. An immoral wealth. Within this long short story, Fitzgerald expresses all the values that belonged to the society of the time: endless beauties—of women and places—, selfishness, superficiality, ambition, desire for success.

In this story Fitzgerald goes into a territory that is particularly dear to him: judgement and criticism of

American society and values, through touches of sarcasm, satire and scenes that sometimes manage to instill real fear in the reader. Here Scott criticizes wealth as the source of pride, as the worst of demons, which leads people towards their own destruction. Above all, he shows that when the Jazz Age was recently born, and its natural destructive effects seemed to be something most people were unaware of, he was able to frame it and recognize its moral and existential flaws. Something that finally seemed annoying, unpleasant, reluctant. All the consequences of a general habituation.

Fitzgerald in this story perfectly frame the risk to which a life of excesses can lead. At the beginning of the story, when John T. Unger, the protagonist, a young man who lives in a small community in the Midwest, moves near Boston to study in a prestigious *prep-school*, his father, greeting him for the last time, says: "Don't forget who you are and where you come from, and you can do nothing to harm you. You are an Unger—from Hades."

Winter Dreams (published in the collection *All the Sad Young Men*, 1926), one of Fitzgerald's short stories, is commonly considered a sort of first draft of *Gatsby*. Although the context changes, the meaning of the story does not change. A dream, a distant and unreachable desire that destroys the protagonist emotionally.

It's important to pay attention to the date of publication of this story: December 1922. At that time Fitzgerald, in just two years, had already published two very successful novels (*This Side of Paradise,* 1920, and *The Beautiful and The Damned,* 1922) and wanted to write something that had never been seen in American literature. He told Max Perkins that it would be "something extraordinary and beautiful and simple and intricately patterned."[5] And nothing, at the time, was more beautiful and complex but at the same time simple than an intense but illusory love.

This story is set in the fictitious *Sherry Island Golf Club.* In reality it's the prestigious *White Bear Yacht Club,* Minnesota, not far from St. Paul, where Scott and Zelda stayed in the summer of 1921.[6] In the pages of this story, the author manages to deal with the subjects that we will find in a more complex form in his third novel. The nonacceptance of one's social status, therefore the subsequent ambitious quest for success. Falling in love not with a woman but with the ideal of that woman. Finally, as Fitzgerald taught us, disillusionment with that same love.

Although this story, just like *Gatsby,* is not one of his most autobiographical works, it demonstrates Fitzgerald's deep awareness of the boozer generation. Despite the many parties to attend; despite a society less attentive to its real needs and more reckless towards the pleasures of life; despite the money accumulated through an uncontrolled upwardly rising economy, Scott perceived the deep sadness of the youth of the time. We can certainly affirm that sometimes Scott himself was part of that social sadness.

Jacob's Ladder is another significant short story from the 1920s. Published in 1927 in the *Saturday Evening Post*, it deals with themes very close to disillusionment dictated by a feeling, and by the feelings themselves interpreted in an inconsistent and irrational way by the protagonists.

Also in this story we find, as always, a male protagonist, Jacob, and a female one, Jenny. The peculiarity, which will be the pivotal point of the whole story, is the age difference between the two. Jacob is a thirty-three year old man, while Jenny is a young sixteen year old girl, full of dreams and illusions. Two such different ages form two different ways of thinking, two different ways of seeing life, and consequently, two different stories, cannot be reconciled.

All the themes of the Jazz Age are here re-proposed again. The ladder to success which is also that of Fitzgerald's own life, as well as the illusion of our feelings destined to break and leave us overwhelmed.

Jacob helps Jenny launch her film career, and at this first point, they both seem to be aware of where their feelings lie. Jenny is grateful for Jacob's help, but she sees him only as a friend, and Jacob, while aware of his affection for her, decides not to declare his love to Jenny. The two meet again a year later, and Jacob at this point declares his love to the girl, who says she don't feel the same way. They both go on with their lives. When they meet again Jenny is now a grown woman and a successful actress, in love with another man. As much as Jacob is eager to change the course of events, and eager to have declared himself when their friendship was just born, he will have to surrender to fate and live with the choice he made years earlier.

In this story Fitzgerald skillfully analyses the evolution of feelings and the gradual development of human emotions, as well as the consequence of the choices made. An apparently right and even random decision can ultimately be humanly overwhelming. The ladder to which Fitzgerald refers in the title of the story, therefore, is that of each of us, which leads us, step by step, decision by decision, to the development and final version of our existence.

In the final analysis, it's important to dwell briefly on one of the most significant sentences of the story, in which the whole characterization of the story is put by the author. With reference to the protagonist, Fitzgerald writes: "Like so many Americans, he valued things rather than cared about them." In this brief sentence Scott tells us that Americans are predisposed to think in a passive and negative way, rather than on an emotional basis. Fitzgerald, through this consideration, is asking himself—

and leading the reader to ask himself: what a relationship would be if, rather than dedicating ourselves to it as a cold, cynical goal to be achieved—an ideal—we actually commit ourselves to what it really has to offer to us, and then find joy in it?[13]

Another important story to analyze, particularly for Fitzgerald's great autobiographical presence, is *A New Leaf*, published in 1931 in the *Saturday Evening Post*. The publishing period of this story is significant, since it's one of the pivotal periods of the American author's entire literary existence. His relationship with Zelda seemed to go adrift, also due to her increasingly frequent nervous breakdowns, while alcohol was now Scott's favorite drink, to which he's giving up with more and more difficulty. These two aspects are also the most important in the very structure of the story.

A New Leaf is based on three main characters. The female protagonist, Julia Ross, who will become over the pages the desire, ambition and finally the tragedy of one of the two male protagonists, Dick Ragland. The second male protagonist, and antagonist of the first, is Phil Hoffman.

The story is deeply autobiographical, especially in Dick's characterization. The story is set in Paris, where the Fitzgeralds lived extemporaneously in the previous years, and where Dick is well known for being an alcoholic, a person capable of drinking almost wildly to the point of destroying himself. It's precisely alcohol that becomes his main enemy. Julia is in love with him, but after his constant wanderings at night drinking and having fun, she decides to leave him. For this reason, in a moment of lucidity, Dick decides to return to America, taking over his life.

At this point, however, we have to analyze the figure of Phil Hoffman, which in conclusion—thanks and because of his actions and words —makes the figure of Dick almost heroic in the eyes of the reader. An heroism immersed in incoherence and in the incapacity to recover.

As we saw before, at the beginning of the story Julia was developing a relationship with Phil, until she fell in love with Dick and decided to leave him. A natural masculine rivalry was born between the two men. Some time later, during an ocean crossing by ship, Dick dies falling overboard. Phil informs Julia, and aware of her feelings for Dick, he declare that his rival in love was succeeding in his intention to stop drinking, omitting the sad reality. The image of Dick, in the finale of the story, thanks to Fitzgerald's romantic prose, takes on the connotations of a fallen hero as he was taking his life back into his own hands.

In the concluding analysis of this story Fitzgerald strips himself before the reader as perhaps few other times he has done in a such way. He paints and makes visible the connotations of his tormented existence, but he also makes visible the awareness he has never renounced throughout his life. Finally, he finds the opportunity to once again sting the American society of the time. Certainly, optimism and hope are a constant heartbeat throughout the story, but what is never lacking is the illusion of idealism that covers the torment of reality.

5

The American novel

It was Fitzgerald's third book that gave him conflicting emotions and success. When his publisher and the critics approved the novel as a unique masterpiece, the public turned away from this judgement. From here on, a predominant rise in Fitzgerald's literary quality began, and ironically, a descent towards reader appreciation.

The author, originally from the Midwest, but with a predominant attitude towards the East Coast lifestyle, produced an impressive work of introspective analysis of the values of American society, and destined the book to the most prestigious literary critics of the decades—and of the following century.

He was able to analyze the inconsistent and incoherent values of the 1920s with extraordinary accuracy. Everything started from a literary aspect dear to Scott: money, and its difference—moral in particular—between those of the old and the new rich. He then went on to the most chaotic and lavish parties and the most frivolous and intangible human relationships. Fitzgerald was able to understand the rampant generational discomfort of those years, and he never told it so well in the book that became known as *The Great Gatsby*.

According to Matthew J. Bruccoli, the most important scholar of Fitzgerald's life and literature, his vision of the 1920s was "serious and complex." He was an integral part of it but at the same time rejected it; he felt outrage at the moral superficiality in which he lived. "He recognized the glamour as well as the waste, the charm as well as the self-destruction."[1]

In the three years that it took him to finish the novel, Fitzgerald developed an increasingly mature awareness that the moment of life we live in immediately becomes part of the past, posing behind us. A concept that then made a cornerstone of the entire book.

What he really wanted to do was to write the American novel. Something that expressed the essence, fragrance and fervor of the country in those years. Not simply a book that would produce excellent criticism, but would include the most intense meaning of American living.

When the Jazz Age was at its peak Fitzgerald was no longer just a capable writer, but artistically mature. He knew he was capable of writing what he later described to Perkins as "the best American novel ever written,"[2] and this awareness belongs only to the greatests. His own editor told him that he had "every kind of right to be proud of this book. It is an extraordinary book, suggestive of all sorts of thoughts and moods."³ A right analysis that goes to touch in depth the true essence of the novel. From Gatsby's incoherent dream to Tom and Daisy's superficiality and moral arrogance. From Jordan's inconsistency and frivolity to Nick's final rejection and contempt for all those who took advantage of Gatsby's astonishing willingness. An intricate map of moods and human relationships.

A fundamental aspect of the book is the narrating voice chosen by the author: Nick Carraway. Continuing the reading of the book it's evident that this character wears the clothes of Fitzgerald himself more than any other. This can be seen in one of the most emblematic and representative sentences of the book, which perfectly describes Nick's state of mind, which was evidently also that of his creator.

In the second chapter, during the scene in the city apartment with Tom Buchanan, Myrtle Wilson and other secondary characters, Nick remembers how:

"High over the city our line of yellow windows must have contributed their share of human secrecy to the casual watcher in the darkening streets, and I was him too, looking up and wondering. I was within and without, simultaneously enchan-

ted and repelled by the inexhaustible variety of life."4

Through Nick, Scott says he belongs to that exclusive, elitist, partying world. A world that at the same time nauseated and disgusted him for the lack of concrete values, something real to lean on, and not fictitious and transient.

Brian Railsback recalled that Scott "when he was sober, he was incredibly aware." He understood the state of well-being, the rich and the richness, but he didn't spare himself in criticizing the destructive effects it could lead to. "While he enjoyed life among the rich and at times was lord of the party during the Jazz Age, a term he is credited with, he was also a deeply moral man (influenced by the Catholic church)."

Through Nick Carraway, said Railsback, Scott said he "could be part of a group but at the same time out of it—he was able to be an insider and an outsider at the same time."

Towards the end of the novel there's a new sentence wrote by the American author from which we can understand all the reluctance, indignation, aversion, that in conclusion Nick, therefore Fitzgerald, felt for that world of corrupt wealth. "They're a rotten crowd," Nick told Gatsby in what was his last conversation with him. It was followed by what Nick described as the only compliment he paid him: "You're worth the whole damn bunch put together." 5

Although *Gatsby* is certainly his least autobiographical novel, the two examples above are a concrete autobiographical tribute of the American author.

In this novel Fitzgerald was not only the writer but the final judge of the story, in an extraordinary mechanism of introspective analysis. "*The Great Gatsby* was the perfect construction of his technique of being inside and outside," Railsback recalled.6

What positively impressed Max Perkins at the first reading of the book was his author's ability to insert into the novel short and concise sentences that were intended to reproduce the concepts and thoughts of American life.

A fundamental place for understanding the story, and an important crossroads even for its development, is the so-called "valley of ashes." Halfway between West Egg, where there are Gatsby's huge mansion, Nick Carraway's small cottage and the homes of the new rich, and the glittering city of New York. In this place, which to the reader's eyes appears sad, dusty and full of human toil and sweat, Fitzgerald puts in an extraordinary masterpiece. A huge billboard that stands out high above the entire valley, reproducing two eyes—those of Dr. T.J. Eckleburg. Eyes that see and observe everything, that appear to the reader as a constant, and sometimes even heavy and oppressive presence—like the eyes of God.

But what makes *The Great Gatsby* in the common imagination the novel that more than any other represents
the search for desire, dream and American opportunity is
an inanimate but constant object in Jay Gatsby's own
thought. The green light at the end of the pier of Daisy
Buchanan's villa, beyond the bay. It's from that light that
everything matches, takes meaning, is fortified. Daisy is
Gatsby's impossible love. So dreamed and desired that he
makes that image even unreal, utopian. Daisy, Fitzgerald
says, is the American dream. The American dream of Jay
Gatsby. And that green light that Gatsby sees across the
bay is the path to that dream. As long as he saw it, he had
reason to believe he could reach it. That light was much
more than what it appeared. It was the beacon that lit the
course in the night.

But, as Fitzgerald taught us, human illusion is the
most predominant aspect of his literature. The relationship between Gatsby and Daisy has never been concrete
or real. There has never been a shared project of life together. It was just a fragment broken by the course of their
existence. This is why Nick Carraway, the narrator of the
story, explains to the reader how for Gatsby "his dream
must have seemed so close that he could hardly fail to
grasp it." Without realizing "that it was already behind
him."7

The extraordinary brilliance of this book is right here.
Fitzgerald gives his generation, and all future generations,

the final perception of life: what we are, what we would like to be and what we would like to be again.

The Great Gatsby was more than a "splendid novel" according to Max Perkins: it was a "wonder." A novel containing "vitality to an extraordinary degree and glamor," but above all "a great deal of underlying thought of unusual quality."[8] This was an aspect that his editor analyzed more deeply. "The amount of meaning you get into a sentence, the dimensions and intensity of the impression you make a paragraph carry, are most extraordinary."[9] He explained that the way he described the characters and the most important places in the book— including the Valley of Ashes and Gatsby's house—were aspects that made a man famous.

According to Perkins, however, at first Gatsby looked like a character with blurred, foggy outlines, not totally comprehensible to the reader. For this reason, through his advices, Fitzgerald was able to make him less vague, more concrete, real and tangible. Another character, however— Tom Buchanan—according to Perkins, was so well described that, he said, if he met him on the street he would have avoided him.

In November 1924, when the book was in its final phase, Perkins wrote to Scott, congratulating him, with admiration and pride for that immense work, not only of writing, but of thought and analysis. "You once said that writing doesn't come <u>naturally</u> to you—my God! You have plainly mastered the craft, of course, but you needed far more far more than craftsmanship for this."[10]

The writing of *The Great Gatsby* as we know it today, in its final version, was not only Fitzgerald's most important literary production, but an intellectual collaboration with his editor. Max Perkins remained convinced throughout his life that the book belonged to the author. That his work was simply to give awareness to the writer so that he could better express the story. So he did with Scott during the developing of Gatsby's story. Yet Perkins remained one, if not the most important and constant supporter of Fitzgerald. From the early days of *Paradise*, theirs always remained a correct cooperation, even psychological to Scott's turbulence life, which soon became friendship, admiration and trust. In his editor, Scott found much more than that. He found understanding and support.

6

The years in France

In Fitzgerald's psychological, and consequently literary, construction, Paris and the French Riviera play a fundamental role. It was here that he knew and developed intricate relationships with many other American expatriates, and it was here, above all, that he understood the scenic power that France—and Europe—could offer to his literature.

Everything started in Paris—artistic, literate, eventful city. Paris—and France—according to Scott Fitzgerald were what America should have been at the time, but was not: the cultural center of every well-thinking American. Walking those streets with outdoor cafés was the best expression of art. "The best of America drifts to Paris. The American in Paris is the best American" he said in 1927. "It is more fun for an intelligent person to live in an intelligent country."

Glossy richness, disillusioned young people and bored

conversations: the flaws that Fitzgerald reproached to America, were also the greatness of his literature. Once again Scott found himself both inside and outside the exciting rhythm of life.

"France has the only two things toward which we drift as we grow older—intelligence and good manners."[1] Paris was beautiful, elegant, sophisticated, intelligent but not pretentious, bold but not vulgar, and for Scott it soon became synonymous of home.

In particular it's the French Riviera that has been a significant place in its character and literary development. The Fitzgeralds arrived in France in 1924 and it didn't take much for them to settle in and fall in love with the warm, clear, welcoming and lively French Riviera. In 1926, at the height of their French years, they rented a villa overlooking the crystal clear sea: *Villa St. Louis*. A few years later, in 1929, it was enlarged with forty rooms and became a five-star hotel, the *Belles-Rives*.

The two years spent on the Riviera, in Antibes, with sporadic interludes in the fascinating and artistic French capital, were defined by Fitzgerald as the happiest of his life. The place where he could let his thoughts and talent flow freely. In 1926 Scott wrote to one of his recent friends, Ernest Hemingway, explaining all the affection he felt for those places. "With our being back in a nice villa on my beloved Riviera (between Nice and Cannes) I'm happier than I've been for years." Looking deeper into the matter, he added, "It's one of those strange, precious and all too transitory moments when everything in one's life seems to be going well."[2]

France has been a place of pleasure and fun for the Fitzgeralds, but also of doubts, reservations and shadows in their relationship. In the course of their marriage, Scott and Zelda were also been envious of each other, contrasting and contradictory people. They drank, had fun, were bored, were in love the moment before and then were jealous of each other because they were both ambitious. A sort of emotional shake that later created and developed the theatrical collapse of their relationship.

In the early 1930s, when they both returned from Europe, Zelda's first real nervous breakdown officially took place. However, over the decades, of numerous historical researches and published books, it has been proven that Zelda had more or less significant and constant nervous breakdowns, even during their years in France.

There is a story in particular, reported by several authors, that seems to demonstrate the first signs of instability by the first American flapper, and to fortify the sad and romantic myth of the couple symbol of jazz, which occurred during their first year on the Riviera. The Murphys play a pivotal role in this story.

During that summer Gerald and Sara Murphy stayed

at the *Hotel du Cap* when, one night, a frantic and shaking Scott Fitzgerald, holding a candle, knocked on their door. Scott had driven almost 30 miles and was obviously worried. He immediately told his friends that his wife had taken an overdose of sleeping pills. "Zelda is sick," he said, then added, "I don't think she did it on purpose." (Whether or not Zelda actually attempted suicide that night is not certain). The three of them then headed to the villa where the Fitzgeralds were staying. Once there, Sara Murphy took Zelda with her, making her walk "up and down, up and down, to keep her from going to sleep." The situation was particularly bizarre. Sara told Zelda to get some olive oil, which would help her vomit. Zelda's response was as absurd as ever: "Sara... don't make me take that, please. If you drink too much oil you turn into a Jew."

According to the authors Nancy Milford and Linda Wagner-Martin, the four friends, after that night, never spoke of it again, with the hope, presumably, that it was a sporadic event, that they could quickly forget it. So obviously did not happen. Another author, Sally Cline, said that it wasn't until forty years later, when the Fitzgeralds had long since died, that the Murphys came back to talk about that episode.[3]

In 1926 the friendship between Scott and the Murphys become less and less transparent and spontaneous, and increasingly ambiguous. Scott's interest in Sara was always particularly evident, from the dawn of their friendship, but in the last period he seemed to have strayed from that and approached an increasingly insistent and overwhelming infatuation. This may have also been a mechanism to make Zelda jealous, but although the American flapper was famous for her jealousy outbursts, she never seemed to be jealous of her friend. Scott would often and annoyingly repeat, "Sara, look at me!" in an attempt to capture her attention, or perhaps Zelda's attention.

Scott had always had a deep admiration for Gerald, however, for what he called natural elegance in his character. All of this could, of course, be scenic material. The American poet and writer Archibald MacLeish recalled that "Scott used to ask Gerald for advice on literary matters."[4]

When we talk about the Fitzgeralds we never talk about them as two separate people, but inexorably connected entities—for better or for worse, in success or tragedy. Partners in drinking and excesses and rivals in love and literature. It's opinion of this writer that Scott Fitzgerald would not have existed without Zelda Sayre. Zelda Sayre would not have existed without Scott Fitzgerald.

Brian Railsback said that "she was an aspiring artist

(dancer, painter, writer)" and consequently "professionally became a kind of rival to Scott."

"Worse, it encouraged him to have fun, to live a high standard of living, but at the expense of his ability to write."[5]

If both of them, Scott and Zelda, went through an emotional, social and artistic collapse in their lives, it's the opinion of this writer that it was because of the behavior of both of them. They were both jealous of the success of the other, they wanted to be painted as the greatest exponents of that era, sometimes even at the expense of the health of their relationship. They were at the same time complementary and distant.

The attention she and her husband paid to themselves was the literary and social oxygen they needed. It was what kept them alive and what later led to their destruction.

Gerald Murphy said of Zelda: "And the strange thing was that no matter what she did—even the wildest, most terrifying things—she always managed to maintain her dignity." But most of all, he said, certainly with the affection of a friend, but also with the knowledge of one of the person closest to them: "She was a good woman, and I never thought she was bad for Scott, as other people said."[6]

7

Tender is the Night

From their earliest days in Europe, the Fitzgeralds used to attend the glittering parties organized by the Murphys in their luxurious house in Antibes, known as *Villa America*. It was from here that Scott found an important source of inspiration for the writing of his fourth novel.

Starting with the Murphys, Fitzgerald drew the protagonists of *Tender is the Night*. But if the character and physical aspect was based on them, the emotional and relational development was clearly based on Scott and Zelda themselves. Fitzgerald certainly took inspiration from the conversations and relational life of his friends, as Gerald Murphy himself noted many years later. From there Scott laid the foundation for the entire novel. As Scott wrote to Murphy, his new book was a work of inspiration, but that inspiration came from his friends. He was terribly fascinated by their life, probably because he saw himself in them. "The second part of the book is completely dedicated to Zelda and me." The reason, he explained, was that "Zelda and I are actually you and Sara."[1] Four people, two complementary couples, but at the same time tremendously different in their view of life.

The Murphys were party planners because no decade like the 1920s allowed them to do this in style, but they were an elegant, sophisticated couple with distinct and refined manners. The Fitzgeralds were imaginative, rebellious and artistic—both. Literary artists and social artists.

In the beginning of the book, when Fitzgerald spoke of the *Hotel des Etrangers*, he referred to a prestigious hotel in Antibes, the *Hotel du Cap-Eden-Roc*. A favorite place for the most important artistic and social personalities of the time. From the Murphys who stayed here during the renovation of their *Villa America*, to Scott and Zelda. But there were many people who stayed here, watching the sea surrounded by Mediterranean pines and immaculate gardens. From Picasso to Hemingway to Dorothy Parker to Gertrude Stein. Even the Kennedy family was a guest here during their social rise. It's therefore easy to understand how much Scott was inspired by such a context. It was the place of excess and pleasure, exuberance and diversity. As Fitzgerald wrote at the beginning of the novel, the *Hotel du Cap* at the time was a "summer resort of notable, fashionable people."[2]

In 1929, when the Fitzgeralds had left their beloved

Riviera and returned to the United States, Scott was working harder and harder on his novel and the Murphys figure was increasingly present in the overall structure of the book. Scott would intrude into his friends' conversations, trying to notice new details to be used in the story. "He kept asking things like what our income was, and how I had got into *Skull and Bones*, and whether Sara and I had lived together before we were married," Gerald recalled. The idea that Fitzgerald could actually use their story as the basis of the novel seemed unreal but in fact increasingly concrete.

Among the Murphys, it was Sara who was most annoyed by this intrusive attitude from her friend. One night, during a party, she couldn't take it anymore. "Scott," she said, "you think if you just ask enough questions you'll get to know what people are like, but you won't. You don't really know anything at all about people." That's when Scott became furious and stood up, pointing his finger at her, telling her that no one had ever dared tell him anything like that. And Sara told him if he wanted to hear her say it again. So she did.

Shortly after that, Sara wrote Scott a note to clarify the situation. She told him that a friendship should not be studied, otherwise it could not be considered a true friendship. At his age, told Sara, he had to live out his friendships, not have theories about them. In a later note she was even more explicit, but visibly interested in clarifying with a friendship she cared deeply about. "We have no doubt of the loyalty of your affections (and we *hope* you haven't of ours) but consideration for other people's feelings, opinions, or even time is *completely* left out of your makeup." She explained to him that his problem in certain situations was that he thought too much about himself, and this even affected his relationship with Zelda and little Scottie. "I feel obliged in honesty of a friend to write you: that the ability to know what another person feels in a given situation will make—or ruin—lives. Your infuriating but devoted and rather wise old friend, Sara."[3]

When *Tender is the Night* was published in the spring of 1934 seemed to be no particularly direct reference to the Murphys. Certainly, Fitzgerald put in places they frequented and took inspiration from conversations made by them and character's aspects, but this novel appeared more than any other the most authentic autobiography of Scott and Zelda's lives.

Fitzgerald's first and last books are also those with more autobiographical references, but they differ profoundly in the basis on which they develop.

This Side of Paradise sees a young man, Amory, and the collegiate life of the early jazz years as its main protagonist. A context in which Scott Fitzgerald narrated himself and his post-graduate life in the form of a novel.

Tender is the Night sees a woman, Nicole, and her husband, Dick, beside her. Zelda's role in this last book is much more predominant and incisive. The author Sally Cline has a clear picture of this, explaining that: "She was a woman who adored and hated her husband, who adored and oppressed and victimized her. Her melodramatic life was in real terms the stuff of fiction." And it's based precisely on this description that the book develops. Fitzgerald tells the reader about the rivalry between him and his wife. An emotional, social, even cultural and certainly literary rivalry, due to the publication of Zelda's book in 1932, which contained material Scott wanted to use for himself. The author Erika Robuck, in fact, explained that "Scott told her that their life together was his material. He used material from her diaries and letters."[4]

This, logically, encouraged an increasingly fierce competition between the couple. Something that led them to the destruction of their relationship and above all of what had made thousands of Americans dream, fall in love and deceive them in previous years: the idea of happiness. Passenger, fleeting, elusive and illusory.

In the summer of 1930 Scott wrote a long letter to Zelda, who was hospitalized at the time. He consciously explained to her why both of them had reached that point in their lives and their inability to sustain their relationship. The role played by literature, friendships, rivalries, Paris and France. But in that letter, as always with Zelda, Scott stripped himself completely naked, showing tenderness, affection, nostalgia, romance and passion.

Fitzgerald proved to be a mature man in understanding their feelings, and he concluded that letter by explaining to her that "we ruined ourselves," but "I have never honestly thought that we ruined each other."[5]

8

The crack up and the recovery

In 1934, back from France, about to finish writing his fourth novel, which took him nine years of his work as a writer, Scott Fitzgerald seemed to be largely forgotten by the American public.[1] Not even the publication of *Tender is the Night* in the spring of that year seemed to relaunch the sales of his books, which were merciless and contributed to the Fitzgeraldian collapse.

Shortly after the publication of the novel, in his obsessive search for a consensus that seemed not to come, he wrote a letter to Hemingway in which he asked him for an honest opinion. "For God's sake drop me a line and tell me one way or the other." All Scott was looking for was a "intelligent opinion" that wasn't "the reviewers' jargon."[2]

America, which had crowned Fitzgerald as the king of the previous decade, had him with the same speed and superficiality rejected into oblivion. The literary style of Scott's early years had shifted from a discerning sarcasm and constant critical irony towards the society of the time that America liked so much, to a darker, sadder and melancholy literature that was rejected by American readers.

In 1937 Scott Fitzgerald's life was at a crossroads—emotional and literary. At the time he was drinking constantly—he was an alcoholic. Despite this, he tried, albeit with difficulty, lucidly and consciously, to take his life back into his own hands.

Her beloved Zelda was admitted to a mental hospital near Asheville, North Carolina. For the two previous summers Scott lived in a nearby hotel to be close to her: The Grove Park Inn. Those were dark and complicated years. Fitzgerald tried, often unsuccessfully, to regain strength from his own emotional collapse, aggravated by an increasingly precarious physical health (at that time he suffered from tuberculosis and the air of the surrounding mountains helped him to recover). Above all, he tried to get his writing back in his hands.

For this reason, in Asheville, Fitzgerald hoped to regain his lost literary splendor. "He came to the Grove Park Inn and chose these rooms (one for writing and one for sleeping) so he could watch the main entrance," Brian Railsback recalled. The very entrance to the luxurious hotel seemed to be the door to the rediscovery of his writing. "He could see the cars coming in and he could see if there was any interesting woman who might look single and what she was wearing."3 Above all, Fitzgerald was looking for a protagonist. Someone rich, charming and seductive. And he was looking for him among the hotel guests.

Most of all, Scott was a lonely man at the time. He was sad for a literature that did not seem to be going as he had hoped; for a life that seemed to have drifted drastically away from his own hands; all seasoned with the terrible feeling and fear of being forgotten by his audience.

In 1934 he wrote a letter to his friend and journalist Henry L. Mencken, specifying that "I would rather impress my image (even though an image the size of a nickel) upon the soul of a people than be known"4 Scott believed that literature was part of human artistic expression, he did not necessarily see it as a career. He had an extremely romantic view of literature. For him the most important thing was to know that what he wrote had value—social and cultural value.

When he realized that his books were no longer in the bookstores, he sent himself a letter in which he tried to reconcile his doubts and fears. A letter full of painful and oppressive words.

"Dear Scott - How are you? Have been meaning to come in and see you. I have [been] living at the Garden of

Allah. Yours, Scott Fitzgerald."

The desperation dictated by an audience that seemed to have abandoned him took over, especially when he was drunk. He would introduce himself to people, hoping to be recognized. "I'm F. Scott Fitzgerald. You've read my books. You've read *The Great Gatsby*, haven't you? Remember?"[5] But America seemed not to remember, or consciously not want to remember.

In 1937, trying to recover from excessive alcohol consumption, work more consistently and rediscover his literature, he moved from the East Coast to the West and the lights of Hollywood cinema.

Publishers seemed to have lost interest in his writing and the reason was that Scott Fitzgerald was expected to write a certain kind of stories. Young people in love, disappointed and bored with life, parties and frantic taxi rides in search of new opportunities. Scott instead wanted to prove to himself that he was much more than just the Jazz Age writer. He wanted to prove he could be versatile, innovative and chameleonic.

"It isn't particularly likely that I'll write a great many more stories about young love. I was tagged with that by my first writings up to 1925" Fitzgerald wrote in 1939 to Kenneth Littauer, *Collier's* editor. He explained that his stories were gradually becoming less and less honest, and increasingly difficult to write. "I think I am much wiser in not trying to strain for it but rather to open up a new well, a new vein." He concluded the letter by consciously explaining that: "Nevertheless, an overwhelming number of editors continue to associate me with an absorbing interest in young girls—an interest that at my age would probably land me behind bars."[6] And California was so different, full of gold and opportunities, and might have been the right way to go.

He signed a contract with *MGM* for $1,000 a week, which was then expanded to $1,250—a more than honorable salary during the Depression. This shows that the interest in him may have faded, but it was not completely disappeared. Scott began his new—and last—ascent from here.

In Hollywood he produced a massive amount of literary and scenic material. Notes and drafts, written and rewritten several times, many of them by hand. For Fitzgerald, Hollywood represented a rebirth. He once again learned to impose a rhythm of daily writing and gradually stopped drinking, almost entirely. Matthew Bruccoli recalled in an interview that there is this distorted idea that during the last years of his life Scott was overwhelmed by drinking and literary vagrancy that didn't produce much, when in fact: "He took screenwriting very seriously." He went on to say, "it's heartbreaking to see how much effort he put into it."[7] Not that the scripts he produced were very successful, but what mattered was the change. Fitz-gerald gradually returned from oblivion and the torment of being done. He never stopped believing in his talent and his ability to come back as a great writer. Probably when he called his life "epic grandeur" he was referring to that too. If his literature overcame his death, one of his greatest human achievements—which did not spare him a mocking farewell—was precisely the way he faced the last three years of his life.

Despite the money earned in cinema, Scott's expenses seemed excessive and endless. In 1939, the rights to all his books earned him only thirty-three dollars.[8] He learned to live humbly, but he wanted the best for his family, ho-wever complicated the situation might be. He paid for Zelda's hospitalization at the best institutions in the country; he paid for his daughter Scottie's education at Vassar College—one of the most prestigious colleges in America. She couldn't always afford all these expenses, so his friends, including the Murphys, came to his side. "I wish we could feel we'd done you a service instead of ma-king you feel some kind of torment," Gerald wrote him. Loyalty, trust and mutual respect, in Scott Fitzgerald's life, was the invisible thread that deeply bound their rela-tionship, and it never wavered. Until the end, Scott was able to count on the affection of his friends. In 1940 he thanked the Murphys for their continued support to him: "There was many a day when the fact that you and Sara did help me seemed the only pleasant human thing that had happened in a world where I felt prematurely passed by and forgotten."9 In his last time in Hollywood Scott was not always successful at work, nor was he always able to give up alcohol—which he often replaced by drinking Coke—but he was no longer a lonely man. He was no longer alone, and he learned to be happy.

While he was in California he started a new book, with an autobiographical touch about his experience in cinema, and the golden image and awareness that Hollywood was recreating and shaping a new America in its image. That book would later be entitled *The Last Tycoon*. Shortly before his death he wrote about one hundred and fifty pages of a manuscript that he wanted to keep no longer than 70,000 words. He produced an enormous amount of sketches and notes, in particular on how he wanted to conclude the book. Notes that helped Edmund Wilson, in 1941, just after Scott's death, finish and then publish the last Fitzgeraldian tribute to America. It's the common opinion of many literary critics that the words of *The Last Tycoon* are among the deepest and most moving words he ever wrote.10

In Hollywood he also found someone with whom he spent the last three years of his life. Sheilah Graham, a columnist who talked about Hollywood gossip in its golden age, and who then developed a love affair with Scott. She helped him to recover from alcohol, to give a rigor to his life that he had previously lost. She was part of the source from which the American author has gradually recovered.

Despite this, his affection for Zelda never changed. They were still married and never gave up writing letters to each other. Brian Railsback noted that in the late 1930s, "Scott and Zelda still loved each other, but they knew that their relationship could not work."[11] Eleanor Lanahan recalled that Zelda wrote "beautiful letters to Scottie about him." Until the end, there is always been understanding, support and awareness between them. In fact, as Lanahan recalled, "even in the darkest times", Scott never stopped to love her, and consider her a fundamental part of his life. "The tenderness is the point," Lanahan fondly said, "that survived everything."[12]

9

Epilogue

The morning of December 21, 1940 was bright and sunny. The temperature was pleasant, and for Scott it was a perfect Californian day to continue working on chapter six of his new book. Fitzgerald was in Sheilah Graham's apartment, eating a candy bar and reading a story about American football in his university newspaper: *Princeton Alumni Weekly*. He must have particularly liked the article, as he was taking notes on the margins of the page. One of them—the last words he ever wrote—was a compliment to the author's writing: "Good prose."[1] He was taking a break from work—he was happy and optimistic about the continuation of his novel. Around 2 p.m. he got up from his armchair, tightened his chest, struggling to breathe, and shortly afterwards fell helplessly onto the floor beside the fireplace. He never got up again.[2]

Scott Fitzgerald was only forty-four years old when he

died, in the most ironic and mocking fate, leaving behind the greatness of his literature and the immensity of his life and character.

Immediately after his death, there were a series of phone calls. His agent Harold Ober, after being alerted by Miss Graham, alerted Perkins, who in turn wired Zelda.

The funeral was a tragic and solitary moment, the last farewell to the man who consciously accepted suffering as a necessity to conquer an ideal, to achieve an ambition. Gerald and Sara Murphy, his friend, mentor and editor Max Perkins and a few other friends attended. Zelda was not there, as the doctors said it was too much psycho-physical effort for her.

Mrs. Bayard Turnbull, a friend of the Fitzgeralds, remembered that Perkins looked lost and disoriented that day. "He didn't say a word to anyone." It was as if he was trying to understand how, why. "Several times, without even paying attention to what was going on, he shook his head, lifted it slowly, and looked at the sky."[3] Almost as if he wanted to find hope in the light, the course that could mark the way, which Scott skillfully described in *The Great Gatsby*.

Only a handful of people attended his funeral. Apparently even his death did not seem to reawaken that tired and selfless part of America. "When he died no one went to the funeral," recalled Dorothy Parker, one of the few people present. "not a single soul came, or even sent a flower." At that moment, Mrs. Parker, a literary colleague and party companion, said quietly in reference to Scott, "Poor son of a bitch." In the moments that followed, some of the present in the room thought it was one of her typical wisecrack. It wasn't. It was a sentence that Scott himself put in *The Great Gatsby* after the main character died. Two months after Fitzgerald's death, writer Glenway Wescott rightly felt that the American author "in the twenties, his heyday, he was a kind of king of our American youth."[4] For this reason, Parker's was the last tribute to the man crowned king by one generation and sadly forgotten by the next.[5]

It's painful to think that in August 1940, when Scott received his last check with the royalties from his books, it only had on it the modest and sad amount of $13.13, with only forty copies sold. Most of them bought by the author himself. It's not true, as has often been said, that at his death his books were out of print. *Scribner* had six of his literary productions in his stores, ready to be sold. The even more tragic truth is that no one seemed to be interested anymore.[6]

In 1946, when America was rediscovering Scott Fitzgerald, Perkins spoke in front of a group of people about his work as an editor, the meaning he gave to this word and his past work with great literary men. That was the first time he spoke in front of students, putting himself—the editor—in front of the one he always believed to be the most important person to protect: the writer. The first question that came out of the audience was, "What was it like to work with F. Scott Fitzgerald?"

Perkins stopped for a moment to think, a fragile, delicate smile broke on the inflexibility of his face, and then said, "Scott was always the gentleman. Sometimes he needed extra support—and sobering up—but the writing was so rich that it was worth it."

It was so rich, full of emotion, desire and interest in making it as real as possible, that his help, he added, was really simple and minimal, because Scott was always a perfectionist. Despite this he was also very sensitive to criticism, said Perkins, which is why you had to think very carefully about the help you suggested.7

Scott Fitzgerald, above all, was a man of character. Humble in facing his weaknesses and ambitious in accepting his hopes. He was critical and affectionate, he was incoherent and sarcastic, he was superficial and friendly, he was attentive but could be intractable, he was spontaneous and thoughtful in the immediate aftermath. A music box of feelings, as he described them—epic. His existence was the highest representation of the American dream—perfectly understood by him. A mix of reality and illusion, of desire and torment, of search and chase.

The relationship between him and Zelda—joyful, sad, eventful, amusing, artistic—was the source that fed that dream, suddenly broken in the satire of life, just when Scott thought he had overcome it.

His friend and literary rival Hemingway said that with alcohol he became irritable and grumpy, but when he was sober he was so nice and self-deprecating. Their friendship was not always easy, due to almost insurmountable differences in their character and the alcohol that often conditioned their relationship. Hemingway recalled that the fickleness of their friendship went on for years but, "for years too, I had no more loyal friend than Scott when he was sober." [8]

This combination of qualities and contrasts in Fitzgerald's character produced true, authentic and immortal literature. The constant desire to write and to do so as a final necessity to find himself. The desire to do it, above all, to not feel abandoned, but to feel understood in a world that seemed silly, cynical and disinterested. During a conversation with Sheilah Graham about some words written about two hundred and fifty years earlier, Scott expressed his extremely romantic but conscious view of literature. "This is part of the beauty of all literature," he told Miss Graham, whom he called Sheilo. "You discover that your longings are universal longings, that you're not lonely and isolated from anyone. You belong."[9]

Fitzgerald's literary greatness lay in his ability to take

his pain into his own hands. Analyzing it, breaking it down, understanding it, reassembling it and finally forming a sentence, a concept, a story, building the most original, authoritative and genuine American literature. In pain, and in the understanding of it, he found his greatest talent.

For Scott, writing was ambition. The ambition to become, the ambition to conquer, and the ambition to reborn again.

In the abundance of world literature, past and present, one certainty remains: Francis Scott Fitzgerald. He was never a writer defined primarily by his own literature, but by his own existence and the theatrical tragedy of human life. He was splendidly devastating when he wrote and tremendously real when he lived. He was tragically dark in pain and was solemnly effervescent in hilarity, like fireworks in the darkness of a summer night. He was too much—too authentic, too real, too much in life and death.

The writer and friend Gertrude Stein chose to describe him as "the most talented writer of his generation, the one with the brightest flame."[10]

Afterword

During the writing of this book, I had the opportunity to meet several people related to the figure of Francis Scott Fitzgerald. Scholars, simple enthusiasts, part of the team of what is today the Fitzgerald Museum in Montgomery, Alabama, where Scott, Zelda and their daughter Scottie lived for a period in the early 1930s, and where Scott worked on *Tender is the Night*. Among these people there is also Marjie Kirkland.

Marjie is a distant cousin of the great American writer who has been told in these pages. It may therefore be curious and interesting to share her words, opinions and thoughts about Fitzgerald, his life and literature. A new way to further explore one of the most important literary figures of the 20th century, and probably the greatest and most representative writer of his generation. It's for this reason that this afterword will be dedicated to the words that Marjie has kindly agreed to share with me.

Life is made of coincidences—if you like to call them

so. On September 24, 2018, 122 years after the birth of the American author F. Scott Fitzgerald, Marjie Kirkland, a distant cousin of him, went into labor, delivering her baby later in the next day, on September 25, the day of the birth of William Faulkner. The same Faulkner who wrote: "The past is never dead. It's not even past."

Her daughter's first name is anything but random: Keyes. A name derived from the original Keye, the blood-line of those English families who settled on the coast of Virginia in 1698. The 7th grade great-grandfather of Marjie was born in Maryland in 1731, and the Keye became Keyes. In 1754 her 6th great-grandfather, General John Ross Key was born. One of his children—Francis Key—later became famous for writing the American anthem. As she reminded to this author, her family's name has changed generation to generation—Keye, Keyes, Key and Keys.

Francis Scott Fitzgerald—whose full name was Francis Scott Key Fitzgerald—was in fact a distant cousin of the writer Francis Key, and this links these two important American historical figures to Marjie Kirkland.

Exactly as the thoughts of the writer of this book, even Marjie in convinced that to fully understand the human figure of Scott, not only his historical part, is necessary read his letters. "The letters he wrote back and forth with Ernest Hemingway were quite nostalgic and loving." This can looks different from the historical image we have of them today, but, says Marjie: "The two friends were very charming towards each other." All this, probably, like a form of illusion to those difficult times, "maybe just like a modern day social media relationship?"

Here is born an interesting point of conversation: the similarities between today's generation and the '20s. "In today's society everything is short and glamours on the surface just like the '20s. Just like Jay Gatsby himself. Some of us are just floating through life to hide what's beneath the surface." Appearance and waste. 2000s as the '20s.

Talking about exchanges of letters, it's impossible not consider those between Scott and his daughter Scottie. It were filled with affection, sometimes reproach, teachings and always unconditional love. According to Marjie, the letters also tells a lot about the personality of Scott, especially those he wrote to his daughter when she was at the summer camp. One of the most famous, in which Scott lists a number of things to her daughter to worry about, and others according to him not so much important, is so beloved by Marjie that she has printed and framed it in her daughter's bedroom.

The relationship between Scott and his daughter Scottie is essential in the psychological understanding and development of both. The growth and emotional stability of Scottie was derived from the mistakes and lessons of her father, who really committed himself in growing positively his daughter.

Marjie, during our conversation, has brought back the words of Dr. Frank Gogan, one of the Scottie's doctors for brief periods of times throughout the years, that he told her personally. "I remember her to be spunky, flinty, resourceful, kind, funny, intelligent, generous and brave."

It's opinion of Marjie that "F Scott's intention was to make his daughter emotional stable, in which he succeed that very much so."

She also remembered that talking with Gogan she had the impression that the personality of Scottie was very similar to that of Judge Sayre (Zelda's father). "She became a solid woman by witnessing and studying her own parents mistakes." In this case, we have the help of the words of F. Scott to his daughter, in his last letter to her few weeks before he died: "You have two beautiful bad examples for parents. Just do everything we didn't do and you will be perfectly safe."

Marjie remembers me that "my father, Honorable Judge James H. Anderson here in my Montgomery, has played a huge impact on my own life too. Also he happens to be a leader in the Democratic Party. So, as you see the Key genes have a powerful impact on carrying a strong influence in ones personality."

Both, Sayre and Key, have "strong will and smarts. Oh,

and both sides have a very healthy sense of humor."

Then the conversation moved on Scott's literature. "*The Beautiful and the Damned* is one of my favorites," says Marjie. The second book of Fitzgerald "sits comfortably on a small table in our lounge."

Marjie says that the female protagonist of the novel, Gloria Gilbert, "reminds me of the relationship he had with Zelda at certain points."

Much has been said about the autobiographical aspect of the female protagonists of Scott, drawn on the physical and psychological aspect of Zelda. According to Marjie, those descriptions "are way more drawn out in her writings compared to Scott." The reason of this is to be found in the capacity of Fitzgerald to express a concept in a very small amount of words, as we analyzed this aspect in the course of this book. "Scott's ability to use one character or one simple metaphor describes so much more with so little words."

Another aspect to be taken into consideration is the eloquence of Fitzgerald's writing. Marjie on this point says that "Scott's writings are very influenced by his beginnings on writing lyrics to play. All of his books looks like an album to me."

When the conversation moves on the mental breakdowns of Zelda and the possible responsibility of Scott in them, Marjie says that "this is all opinion based" on an extremely sensitive question.

"I'm married to a psychologist, forensic examiner and he see the worst of worst. His father too. My father is a judge. I grew up in politics. My biological mother being an artist moved to New Zealand when I was 5. She suffered with depression and still does. Gosh, there's so much." For this reason, says Marjie to me, try to give an answer on Zelda "it's really hard."

First, trying to analyze the problem, she says: "I don't believe they had the correct medicine for her." The reason was probably due to her artistic skills (she was a good writer, dancer, painter...). "Most artists can remain completely noncreative when they're on the right medicine."

"Terribly real, I've seen it though." However, "Zelda did amazing paintings in rehab."

"Honestly"? says Marjie, "I think she was just bored. And reactive. She was a shaker and a flapper!"

Obviously, also the situation of her family could have contributed to her increasingly frequent nervous breakdowns. "She was sad in her marriage... She had a child and not keep or have children might had changed her esteem of her own self in different areas."

"And who knows what medicine she needed. It wasn't gin." That, of course we know, was the apparent solution to Scott's problems.

The last topic we talked was if she had one or more sentences of Scott or Zelda that she particularly love. About Scott, she said, "it's a toss! Changes weekly. So I will pick one I used last week that spoke loudly."

"*You & I have been happy; we haven't been happy just once, we've been happy a thousand times.*" A letter that Scott wrote to Zelda while she was in hospital, when their marriage was a sinking boat, but not their feelings to each other.

A significant phrase, which, tell us Marjie, has recently helped her to understand what happiness really is. "Happiness is the state of a moment, a still film of time. The more times you get and the more one feels the emotion of calm in reaction." Some kind of endless addiction. Happiness bring happiness. "So many people are too afraid to just laugh hard or not feel better. Happiness is happening once, then hopefully more! If I feel happy will it be taken for granted or will I be alone?" Marjie reminds me that it's sad when someone feel bad emotions, loneliness or melancholy, because "happiness is just there for you like a mother to a child, a bird to a tree or the simple sound of a bell." You need to search and find happiness because "it can just keep happening a thousand more times!"

Thinking about what Scott would wanted to say to Zelda in the above mentioned quote, says Marjie, it could be something like: *We've been happy a thousand times Zelda. You don't need anger or sadness for attention.*

"That's how he's speaking to me in this quote to her."

AKNOWLEDGMETS

This writing work is been my first book published in Italy, and I am happy to see it go on its way on the English market.

I deeply thank Valentino Corino, a good friend, for the help with the editing, suggestions and constant support from my first days of writing. Roberto Rossi, a friend and a good writing fellow. Alessandro Arcuri, a friend and a talented writer, for giving me the idea to translate this book and for believe in my work. Sonia Zenucchi, a friend who beautifully made me a happier person. Cindy Stroud Reddick, Dusty Richard and Mark Chekares who never stopped to believe in me, in what I am doing, even when the distance could have made this difficult. They are special person, and good friends. Marjie Kirkland, for the interest in my work, for the constant availability to share with me her thoughts and suggestions about this topic and for her wonderful words I put in the afterword of this book. Julian McPhillips, founder of the Fitzgerald Museum, for the interest in my work with the goal to share and promote the story of the Museum and the Fitzgeralds through my personal blog and this publication. Brian Railsback, a Fitzgerald scholar, for the kind availability to be interviewed. And my parents, of course, Tiziana Schena and Bruno Brignoli, to constantly support me through this process.

ABOUT THE AUTHOR

Tiziano Brignoli is previously author of four Italian books, the most important of which is a biography about President Kennedy's life and character. At the moment he is working on new projects, both fiction and non-fiction. He love hike in the wilderness, and lives in a little town in the Italian Alps.

You can find him at:
www.tizianobrignoli.it
www.storiesaboutamerica.com

BIBLIOGRAPHY

INTRODUCTION

1 Sarà un capolavoro by F. Scott Fitzgerald, edited by Leonardo G. Luccone, pag. 14

2 How to live on practically nothing a year/How to live on $36000 a year by F. Scott Fitzgerald

3 A life in letters by F. Scott Fitzgerald, edited by Matthew J. Bruccoli, pag. 313

4 thoughtco.com "Review: 'Hemingway vs. Fitzgerald'" by Esther Lombardi

5 Sarà un capolavoro by F. Scott Fitzgerald, edited by Leonardo G. Luccone, pag. 280

CHAPTER ONE. A CHARACTER'S PROFILE

1 "Fitzgerald: The Romance of Money" by Malcolm Cowley

2 The Crack Up by F. Scott Fitzgerald, pag. 318, 1964 edition

3 "Fitzgerald: The Romance of Money" by Malcolm Cowley - see also The Crack Up by F. Scott Fitzgerald, pag. 87, 1964 edition

4 The Crack Up by F. Scott Fitzgerald, pag. 69, 1964 edition

5 newyorker.com "Living well is the best revenge" by Calvin Tomkins

6 Author's interview

7 newyorker.com "Living well is the best revenge" by Calvin Tomkins

8 nytimes.com "Scott and Zelda: their style lives" by Eleanor Lanahan

CHAPTER TWO. THE NEW VIBRANT LITERARY VOICE OF THE JAZZ AGE

1 A writer's use of material by Patricia Kane, Minnesota Historical Society
2 "The Author's Apology" by F. Scott Fitzgerald
3 "How that boy Fitzgerald can write!" by Harry Hansen, Chicago News
4 capitalcentury.com "1920: Fitzgerald's own paradise" by Jon Blackwell/The Trentonian
5 The Crack Up by F. Scott Fitzgerald, pag. 17, 1964 edition
6 Author's interview
7 I'd die for you and other lost stories by F. Scott Fitzgerald, edited by Anne Margaret Daniel
8 This side of Paradise by F. Scott Fitzgerald, pag. 46
9 Author's interview
10 "What a Flapper Novelist Thinks of his Wife," The Courier Journal
11 scottandzelda.com
12 "The Age of Epic Grandeur: F. Scott Fitzgerald and America's Cultural Memory of the 1920's" by Nicole McQuiston
13 The Crack Up by F. Scott Fitzgerald, pag. 89, 1964 edition

CHAPTER THREE. NARRATE LIFE

1 "What a Flapper Novelist Thinks of his Wife," The Courier Journal

2 people.com "F. Scott Fitzgerald & Zelda Sayre"

3 nytimes.com "Scott and Zelda: their style lives" by Eleanor Lanahan

4 archive.nytimes.com "Troubled Life and Times on This Side of Paradise" by Michiko Kakutani

5 Everybody was so young by Amanda Vaill, pag. 147

6 pbs.org "The Legend of Zelda (Sayre Fitzgerald)" by Ben Phelan

7 Max Perkins editor of genius by A. Scott Berg, pag. 173, 1979 edition

8 shmoop.com "F. Scott Fitzgerald - The Jazz Age"

9 This side of Paradise by F. Scott Fitzgerald, pagg. 43-45

CHAPTER FOUR. SHORT STORIES

1 theaustralian.com.au "F. Scott Fitzgerald's short stories, biography chronicle troubled life" by Don Anderson

2 independent.co.uk "I'd Die for You and Other Lost Stories by F Scott Fitzgerald, book review" by Alasdair Lees

3 newyorker.com "The lost stories of F. Scott Fitzgerald" by Deborah Treisman

4 theaustralian.com.au "F. Scott Fitzgerald's short stories, biography chronicle troubled life" by Don Anderson

5 forbes.com "Charles Scribner Illuminates F. Scott Fitzgerald's "The Great Gatsby"" by Mary Claire Kendall

6 http://www.wbyc.com

CHAPTER FIVE. THE AMERICAN NOVEL

1 shmoop.com "F. Scott Fitzgerald - The Lost Generation"

2 Max Perkins editor of genius by A. Scott Berg, pag. 63, 1979 edition

3 Ibid, pag. 64

4 The great Gatsby bi F. Scott Fitzgerald, pag. 53

5 Ibid, pag. 152 - Author's interview

6 Author's interview

7 The great Gatsby by F. Scott Fitzgerald, pagg. 174-175

8 Max Perkins editor of genius by A. Scott Berg, pag. 64, 1979 edition

9 Ibid, pag. 66

10 Sarà un capolavoro by F. Scott Fitzgerald, edited da Leonardo G. Luccone, pag. 79 - see also Max Perkins editor of genius by A. Scott Berg, pag. 67, 1979 edition

CHAPTER SIX. THE YEARS IN FRANCE

1 travelandleisure.com "See F. Scott Fitzgerald's Paris, in All Its Jazz Age Glory" by Jess McHugh

2 nytimes.com "On the French Riviera, Fitzgerald Found His Place in the Sun" by Nina Burleigh - see also townandcountrymag "F. Scott Fitzgerald's Favorite Places on the French Riviera" by Nadine Jolie Courtney

3 newyorker.com "Living Well is the best revenge" by Calvin Tomkins - see also jstor.org "Authorship and Artistry" by Christine Grogan - see also Everybody was so young by Amanda Vaill, pag. 147

4 newyorker.com "Living Well is the best revenge" by Calvin Tomkins

5 Author's interview

6 newyorker.com "Living Well is the best revenge" by Calvin Tomkins

CHAPTER SEVEN. TENDER IS THE NIGHT

1 hellomonaco.com "Stranger than fiction"
2 Tender is the Night by F. Scott Fitzgerald
3 newyorker.com "Living Well is the best revenge" by Calvin Tomkins
4 theguardian.com "'Call me Zelda': writers take on troubled life of F Scott Fitzgerald's muse" by Peter Beaumont
5 Sarà un capolavoro by F. Scott Fitzgerald, edited by Leonardo Luccone, pagg. 151-155

CHAPTER EIGHT. THE CRACK UP AND THE RE-COVERY

1 archive.nytimes.com "Gatsby, 35 years later" by Arthur Mizener - see also usatoday.com "F. Scott Fitzgerald's tragic last act" by Kevin Nance
2 Sarà un capolavoro by F. Scott Fitzgerald, edited by Leonardo G. Luccone, pag. 182
3 npr.org "For F. Scott And Zelda Fitzgerald, A Dark Chapter In Asheville, N.C." by Susan Stamberg
4 Sarà un capolavoro by F. Scott Fitzgerald, edited by Leonardo G. Luccone, pag. 180
5 archive.nytimes.com "Gatsby, 35 years later" by Arthur Mizener
6 I'd die for you and other lost stories by F. Scott Fitzgerald, edited by Anne Margaret Daniel

7 nytimes.com "Fitzgerald as Screenwriter: No Hollywood Ending" by Charles McGrath

8 theguardian.com "City of dreams" by David Thomson

9 newyorker.com "Living well is the best revenge" by Calvin Tomkins

10 theguardian.com "City of dreams" by David Thomson

11 Author's interview

12 people.com "F. Scott Fitzgerald & Zelda Sayre"

CHAPTER NINE. EPILOGUE

1 Princeton.edu "The last thing he wrote" by Anne Margaret Daniel

2 pbs.org "F. Scott Fitzgerald's life was a study in destructive alcoholism" by Dr. Howard Markel - see also Max Perkins editor of genius by A. Scott Berg, pag. 389, 1979 edition

3 Ibid, pagg. 389-390

4 theparisreview.org "Dorothy Parker, The Art of Fiction No. 13" by Marion Capron - see also openculture.com "F. Scott Fitzgerald Recites "Ode to a Nightingale"

5 The Crack Up by F. Scott Fitzgerald, pag. 323, 1964 edition

6 Fitzgerald and Hemingway: Works and Days by Scott Donaldson

7 Max Perkins editor of genius by A. Scott Berg, pagg. 6-7, 1979 edition

8 Festa Mobile (A Moveable Feast) by Ernest Hemingway, pag. 123

9 Beloved Infidel: The Education of a Woman by Sheilah Graham e Gerold Frank, pag. 260

10 scottandzelda.com

Printed in Great Britain
by Amazon

62495547R00059